SAINSBU

Quick and Easy
Classic Italian

Aldo Zilli

Contents

Published exclusively for J Sainsbury plc

Stamford House Stamford Street

London SE1 9LL

by Martin Books

Simon & Schuster Consumer Group

Grafton House 64 Maids Causeway

Cambridge CB5 8DD

Published 1997

ISBN 0 85941 951 7

© 1997 Martin Books

Printed and bound in Italy

Design: Moore Lowenhoff

Photography: Steve Baxter

Styling: Jo Harris

Food preparation: Sara Buenfeld

Typesetting: Cambridge Photosetting Services

Pictured on the front cover: Olive Insaporite (Marinated Olives, page 6)

Introduction

When I was first asked to write this book, I started looking at what we, as a family, bought when shopping in supermarkets. Because, when she comes home from school, my daughter wants to eat now and not in an hour's time, my wife and I never have much time to think. As a result, we always choose to buy ingredients that are quick and easy to cook.

Most Italian ingredients are just that but the true secret of the best Italian cooking lies in the freshness of those ingredients, and in imagination. Not so long ago, rocket, sun-dried tomatoes and balsamic vinegars were rare delicacies but now incredibly, you can buy all these ingredients in the supermarket. Olive oils and olives are also available for you to take away and flavour to your liking at home – it's as easy as ABC and I show you how in the recipes that follow. A choice of fresh pasta or dried would also have been unheard of ten years ago: now they're all there and more – it's just brilliant! And as for the ample supplies of bread – foccacia, ciabatta and country rounds – the choice is endless.

I'm also a great believer in making life easy in the kitchen at home and see no reason why I should slave preparing preserved *antipasti* when there are jars and jars of matured, flavoursome garlic mushrooms, sun-dried peppers and artichokes in vinaigrette just waiting to be served. So do not be afraid to reproduce all these recipes at home for you and your family. My Italian cooking really is easy and fast. *Buon appetito*!

RECIPE NOTES

All recipes in this book give ingredients in both metric (g, ml, etc.) and imperial (oz, pints, etc.) measures. Use either set of quantities, but not a mixture of both, in any one recipe. All teaspoons and tablespoons are level, unless otherwise stated.
1 teaspoon = a 5 ml spoon;
1 tablespoon = a 15 ml spoon;
Egg size is medium, unless otherwise stated.
Fruits are medium-sized, unless otherwise stated.

PREPARATION AND COOKING TIMES

Preparation and cooking times are included at the head of the recipes as a general guide; preparation times, especially, are approximate and timings are usually rounded to the nearest 5 minutes. Preparation times include the time taken to prepare ingredients in the list, but not to make any 'basic' recipe. The cooking times given at the heads of the recipes denote cooking periods when the dish can be left largely unattended, e.g. baking, and not the total amount of cooking time for the recipe. Always read and follow the timings given for the steps of the recipe in the method.

FOOD SAFETY ADVICE: RAW EGGS

A number of recipes in this book are made using raw eggs that receive no further cooking. Sainsbury's believes in offering you as wide a variety of foods and recipes as possible, but we would like to remind customers that there is a risk, albeit very low, of Salmonella infection associated with the consumption of raw eggs. If you intend to consume uncooked dishes containing raw eggs, you should ensure that they are as fresh as possible and, ideally, refrigerated after purchase. We strongly advise pregnant women, young children and those individuals particularly susceptible to infection to avoid eating raw or lightly cooked eggs and uncooked dishes containing raw egg.

Antipasti Caldi e Freddi

Hot and Cold Hors d'Oeuvre

Traditionally, *antipasti* were equivalent to 'nibbles': they were served for special occasions, such as weddings and christenings, ready and waiting at the table. *Antipasti* used to be a selection of hot and cold, cooked and raw food – hot or cold vegetables or salads, cured meats such as Parma ham and salami and fresh fruits that included melons or figs. The *antipasti* would then be followed by pasta or a starter, meat and then dessert.

However, the health-conscious Italian public of today would not want to sit through four courses even if they had time to do so; therefore, most *antipasti* now appear as starters on restaurant menus.

Tortino Italiano
Galette of Tomatoes

Preparation and cooking time: 15 minutes.
Freezing: not recommended. Serves 4.

For a substantial lunch, simply make the pastry circle larger and arrange the tomatoes in a fan before grilling. Serve with Rucola e Parmigiano (Rocket and Parmesan Salad, page 26).

250 g (8 oz) puff pastry, thawed if frozen
1 egg, beaten lightly
leaves from 1 pot of fresh basil, chopped finely
4 tablespoons olive oil

4 plum tomatoes
150 g (5 oz) sun-dried tomato paste
sea-salt flakes and freshly ground black pepper

❶ Preheat the oven to Gas Mark 7/220°C/425°F. Thinly roll out the puff pastry on a lightly floured surface. Using a 9 cm (3½-inch) round pastry cutter or mug, stamp out four circles. Place on a baking tray and brush with the beaten egg.

❷ Bake the pastry circles for 5–8 minutes, until well risen and golden brown.

❸ Meanwhile, in a small bowl, mix the basil and oil, cover and leave to infuse until required.

❹ To skin the tomatoes, blanch in a pan of boiling water for 2 minutes. Drain and plunge into cold water. Drain and slip off the skins. Slice the tomatoes widthways. Preheat the grill to hot.

❺ Loosen the puff pastry slightly on the baking tray and flatten the circles slightly. Spread the sun-dried tomato paste on the circles and then top with the sliced plum tomatoes. Spoon over the basil oil and sprinkle with sea-salt flakes and pepper. Cook under the grill for 2 minutes, until heated through. Serve immediately.

Olive Insaporite
Marinated Olives

**Preparation time: 10 minutes + 30 minutes marinating.
Freezing: not recommended. Serves 4.**

A selection of marinated olives is ideal with drinks. It's important to crush the olives first, for flavours to seep through. I love this idea, simply because you can change your dressing as and when you like, depending on the fresh ingredients available.

2 × 454 g cans of green olives, drained

454 g can of black olives, drained

leaves from 1 pot of fresh basil, chopped
   roughly

6 tablespoons chopped fresh flat-leaf parsley

For the Parmesan and Chilli Olives:

2 tablespoons freshly grated parmesan cheese

1 tablespoon crushed chilli flakes

150 ml (¼ pint) extra-virgin olive oil

For the Balsamic Vinegar Olives:

150 ml (¼ pint) extra-virgin olive oil

4 tablespoons balsamic vinegar

For the Garlic Olives:

4 garlic cloves, crushed

150 ml (¼ pint) extra-virgin olive oil

salt and freshly ground black pepper

❶ In three separate bowls, lightly crush the olives and mix in the chopped herbs.

❷ For the parmesan and chilli dressing, mix all the ingredients together and season with salt and pepper. Stir the dressing into a bowl of green olives.

❸ For the balsamic vinegar dressing, mix the oil and vinegar and season with salt and pepper. Mix the dressing into the remaining green olives.

❹ For the garlic dressing, mix the garlic and olive oil in a bowl and season to taste. Stir into the black olives.

❺ Cover all the bowls of olives with cling film and leave to marinate for at least 30 minutes at room temperature.

Verdure al Formaggio
Grilled Vegetables

Preparation and cooking time: 20 minutes.
Freezing: not recommended. Serves 4.

2 courgettes

1 medium-size aubergine

2 chicory heads

2 teaspoons sea-salt flakes

4 tablespoons olive oil

175 g (6 oz) Brie cheese, sliced thinly

2 tablespoons freshly grated parmesan cheese

2 tablespoons balsamic vinegar

freshly ground black pepper

❶ Preheat the grill to medium hot. Thinly slice the courgettes and aubergine, lengthways. Quarter the chicory lengthways. Place all the vegetables on a foil-lined grill pan and sprinkle with the sea salt and pepper. Drizzle with 3 tablespoons of the olive oil.

❷ Cook the vegetables under the grill for 10 minutes, turning once.

❸ Transfer the vegetables to a heatproof serving dish and top with the sliced Brie; drizzle over the remaining olive oil and sprinkle with the parmesan cheese. Return to the grill and cook for 5 minutes, until the cheese melts and turns golden. Drizzle over the balsamic vinegar and serve immediately.

Asparagi al Prosciutto
Fresh Asparagus with Parma Ham

Preparation and cooking time: 20 minutes.
Freezing: not recommended. Serves 4.

Just a few ingredients are needed for this truly classic dish! Make sure not to overcook the asparagus at the beginning of the recipe.

20 jumbo asparagus spears

4 large slices of Parma ham

50 g (2 oz) butter

4 tablespoons freshly grated parmesan cheese

freshly ground black pepper

❶ Peel the asparagus stems, discarding the hard, woody end. Bring a large frying-pan of water to the boil and gently ease the asparagus into the water. Simmer for 5–8 minutes, until the tips are just tender. Preheat the grill to medium hot.

❷ Drain the asparagus and leave to cool slightly. Divide the asparagus into four

bunches of five stalks and then wrap the stems with the Parma ham. Place each parcel on a baking tray.

❸ Add a knob of butter to each bunch and sprinkle with the parmesan cheese and plenty of pepper. Place under the grill for 5 minutes, until the cheese melts. Serve immediately.

Rollatini di Cipolla Ripieni
Baked Onion Parcels

Preparation and cooking time: 30 minutes.
Freezing: not recommended. Serves 4.

This dish is cheap and extremely tasty. Serve as a starter or accompaniment to Fegato al Lardo (Lamb's Liver with Bacon and Caramelised Onions, page 64).

1 large onion
250 g (8 oz) ricotta cheese
125 g (4 oz) pine kernels
500 g (1 lb) young spinach leaves, chopped roughly
leaves from 1 pot of fresh basil, chopped roughly
1 tablespoon freshly grated parmesan cheese

285 g jar of sun-dried tomatoes in oil, drained and chopped
1 tablespoon fresh white breadcrumbs
2 eggs, beaten lightly
1 tablespoon soft brown sugar
1 tablespoon olive oil
salt and freshly ground black pepper

❶ Preheat the oven to Gas Mark 6/200°C/ 400°F. Peel the onion and trim the ends. Stand the onion upright on its root end. Now place the tip of a knife at the top of the onion and cut down, but stop before you reach the root so that the whole thing remains intact; you're not cutting the onion in half – the idea is to cut through each layer of the onion once and once only. Place the onion in a deep pan with enough water to cover. Bring to the boil and simmer for 10 minutes until tender.
❷ Meanwhile, make the stuffing. Place the ricotta cheese in a large bowl and beat in the pine kernels, spinach, basil, parmesan cheese, sun-dried tomatoes,

breadcrumbs and eggs. Season well with salt and pepper and mix to form a paste.
❸ Drain the onion and leave to cool slightly. Gently unfold the layers of onion and separate. Gently lay the largest onion layer on a work-surface. Spread with some of the stuffing, top with the next largest layer and spread that with some stuffing. Repeat until all the layers are used up. Coax the onion layers back into their original shape (they do this very easily). Place on a baking tray, sprinkle over the sugar and then the oil. Bake for 10 minutes, until the sugar begins to caramelise. Serve warm or cold.

Fegatini al Balsamico
Chicken Liver Salad with Balsamic Vinegar

Preparation and cooking time: 15 minutes.
Freezing: not recommended. Serves 4.

Normally, chicken livers are used to make pâté. Why not throw this unusual warm salad recipe together in minutes and, with the minimum of fuss, impress your friends?

500 g (1 lb) frozen chicken livers, thawed

4 tablespoons olive oil

500 g (1 lb) seedless grapes, stalks removed, halved

4 tablespoons balsamic vinegar

200 g (7 oz) mixed salad leaves

salt and freshly ground black pepper

❶ Remove and discard any membranes from the chicken livers and then cut into large pieces. Season the chicken livers with salt. Heat the oil in a frying-pan and add the livers. Cook over a high heat for 5 minutes, until browned on the outside but still pink inside.

❷ Add the grapes and balsamic vinegar to the chicken livers and cook for a further 2–3 minutes. Season to taste with salt and pepper.

❸ Divide the salad leaves between four serving plates and spoon over the chicken livers, ensuring you add all the juices. Serve immediately.

Scamorza al Lardo
Smoked Mozzarella with Bacon

Preparation and cooking time: 10 minutes.
Freezing: not recommended. Serves 4.

Smoked mozzarella is much harder than conventional mozzarella cheese and keeps its shape during cooking. This recipe is a favourite at my restaurant. These grilled bacon-wrapped chunks of mozzarella are especially popular served as nibbles at parties or a barbecue.

4 rashers of unsmoked back bacon, de-rinded

150 g (5 oz) smoked mozzarella or other hard smoked cheese

1 tablespoon olive oil

25 g (1 oz) butter, softened

2 tablespoons freshly grated parmesan cheese

1 tablespoon chopped fresh flat-leaf parsley

mixed lettuce leaves, to serve

❶ Preheat the grill to medium hot. Using the blunt side of a knife, scrape along each rasher of bacon, to stretch it. Cut the mozzarella into quarters and wrap each with bacon. Place on a foil-lined grill pan and sprinkle with the oil.

❷ In a separate bowl, mix together the butter and parmesan cheese. Spoon over the wrapped mozzarella. Cook under the grill for 5 minutes. Sprinkle with the parsley. Place on a bed of crisp lettuce to serve.

Caprino alle Pere
Grilled Goat's Cheese with Poached Pears

**Preparation and cooking time: 15 minutes.
Freezing: not recommended. Serves 4**

Be sure to use goat's cheese that has rind and does not spread everywhere when it's cooked. Alternatively, put the cheese on grilled ciabatta bread for the cheese to melt over.

2 firm pears, peeled
1 tablespoon sugar
juice from ½ lemon
4 × 125 g Somerset goat's cheese

50 g (2 oz) butter
3 tablespoons freshly grated parmesan cheese
freshly ground black pepper

❶ Halve the pears lengthways and scoop out the core and pips with a teaspoon. Place the pears in a large pan, with enough cold water to cover. Add the sugar and lemon juice and gently bring to the boil. Reduce the heat and simmer for 10 minutes until tender; the point of a knife should easily pierce the pear.

❷ Preheat the grill to medium hot. Meanwhile, halve each goat's cheese widthways and place on a baking tray, cut-side up. Top each slice with a little butter and sprinkle with the parmesan cheese. Grill for 5 minutes, until the tops are golden brown.

❸ Drain the pears and pat dry with kitchen paper. Place the pear halves, cut-side down, on a clean surface and thinly slice lengthways but not all the way to the stalk end. Place each pear half on a serving plate and fan out. Top with the goat's cheese and sprinkle with pepper to serve.

Gamberoni alla Diavola
Devilled Prawns

Preparation and cooking time: 15–20 minutes.
Freezing: not recommended. Serves 4.

If you like, use 500 g (1 lb) of peeled prawns in place of the larger Mediterranean prawns. Serve with plenty of crusty bread, to soak up all the delicious juices.

12 shell-on raw Mediterranean prawns, thawed
** if frozen**
2 tablespoons olive oil
1 shallot, chopped finely
2 tablespoons brandy (optional)
2 fresh red chillies, de-seeded and chopped
** finely**
2 garlic cloves, chopped

150 ml (¼ pint) dry white wine
15 g (½ oz) butter
200 g (7 oz) pitted black olives in brine,
** drained and sliced**
3 tablespoons chopped fresh flat-leaf parsley
2 tablespoons chopped fresh coriander
salt and freshly ground black pepper

❶ Cut the prawns in half, lengthways, leaving the tails intact.

❷ In a large frying-pan, heat the oil. Add the shallot and cook for 2–3 minutes, until soft. Add the prawns and cook for 2–3 minutes on each side, until golden. If using, add the brandy and ignite to flambé the prawns; continue to cook for 1 minute, until the flames die down.

❸ Add the chillies, garlic and wine and season with salt and pepper to taste. Simmer for 5 minutes, until the liquid has reduced by half. Stir in the butter, olives and herbs and cook for 2 minutes. Serve immediately.

Crostini Misti
Toasted Italian Bread with a Selection of Toppings

Preparation and cooking time: 25 minutes.
Freezing: not recommended. Serves 4.

The roast pepper and tomato toppings can be prepared well in advance – allowing the flavours to infuse for longer makes them taste even better. Try not to be like me and eat too many while preparing the other courses!

2 red peppers
2 extra-large tomatoes
6 tablespoons olive oil
4 garlic cloves, chopped
1 red onion, chopped finely

leaves from 1 pot of fresh basil, chopped
1 ciabatta loaf, sliced
4 slices of Parma hame
150 g (5 oz) mozzarella cheese, sliced
salt and freshly ground black pepper

❶ Preheat the oven to Gas Mark 6/200°C/400°F. Place the peppers on a baking tray and roast for 15 minutes, until charred all over. Transfer the peppers to a bowl, cover with clingfilm and leave for 10 minutes.

❷ Meanwhile, skin the tomatoes. Blanch the tomatoes in a large pan of boiling water for 3 minutes. Drain and plunge into cold water. Drain again and you should find the skins slip off easily. Roughly chop the tomatoes and mix with half the olive oil and garlic. Mix in the red onion and basil and season with salt and pepper to taste.

❸ Peel and discard the skins from the peppers and then cut them in half. Remove the core and seeds. Place the peppers in a bowl, with the remaining olive oil and garlic, and season with salt and pepper. Leave to marinate for at least 10 minutes.

❹ Meanwhile, toast the ciabatta bread on both sides. Arrange the Parma ham and mozzarella on four slices of the toasted bread. Return to the grill and cook for 2–3 minutes, until the mozzarella is golden and bubbling. Use the tomato and pepper toppings on the remaining toast. Serve immediately.

Insalate, Verdure, Zuppe

Salads, Vegetables and Soups

All the salads and vegetables are excellent accompaniments to the pasta, risotto, meat and fish dishes in the chapters that follow. Many of the vegetables and salads can also be served as starters in their own right: Endive al Dolcelatte (Mixed Endives with Dolcelatte, page 32), Rucola e Parmigiano (Rocket and Parmesan Salad, page 26), Funghi Stroganoff (Flat Mushrooms in Cream and Mustard Sauce, page 28), Spinaci al Lardo (Spinach and Crispy Bacon Salad, page 24), and Patate, Radicchio e Salmone (Potato, Radicchio and Smoked Salmon Salad, page 26).

The soups can either be served as starters or as light lunches or suppers, accompanied by crusty Italian bread.

Stracciatella alla Romana
Egg and Parmesan Cheese Soup

Preparation and cooking time: 25 minutes.
Freezing: not recommended. Serves 4.

My mother always made this soup on Sundays, when all the family gathered, because it's so simple and easy. Once the eggs have been added to the boiling stock, make sure the soup does not boil again or the eggs will curdle.

For the Croûtons:

4 thick slices of white bread, cut into large chunks

2 tablespoons olive oil

3 garlic cloves, crushed

1 tablespoon chopped fresh flat-leaf parsley

For the Soup:

4 eggs

2 tablespoons freshly grated parmesan cheese

2 tablespoons chopped fresh flat-leaf parsley

1 tablespoon single cream

1.2 litres (2 pints) chicken stock

salt and freshly ground black pepper

❶ Preheat the oven to Gas Mark 6/200°C/400°F. Place the bread in a small roasting tin, drizzle with the olive oil and sprinkle over the garlic and parsley. Season with salt and pepper. Bake for 15 minutes until golden brown.

❷ Meanwhile, put the eggs, parmesan cheese, parsley and cream in a large bowl and beat well to mix.

❸ Put the chicken stock in a large pan and bring to the boil. Over the heat, whisk in the egg mixture and season to taste with salt and pepper. Simmer for a further 2–3 minutes, to heat through. Serve immediately, with the garlic croûtons.

Zuppa di Funghi
Mushroom Soup

Preparation and cooking time: 30 minutes.
Freezing: recommended. Serves 4.

The dried porcini have a concentrated flavour and a few go a very long way. It's important to soak the porcini in hot water before using.

10 g bag of dried porcini

75 g (3 oz) butter

1 onion, chopped

1 kg (2 lb) mushrooms, chopped

500 g (1 lb) potatoes, peeled and finely
   chopped

160 g bunch of fresh coriander, chopped

1 tablespoon English mustard

2 tablespoons plain flour

300 ml (½ pint) milk

½ teaspoon freshly grated nutmeg

salt and freshly ground black pepper

chopped fresh coriander, to serve

❶ Place the dried porcini in a large bowl and pour in 150 ml (¼ pint) of boiling water. Leave to stand for 15 minutes.

❷ Meanwhile, put half the butter in a large pan and heat to melt. Add the onion and fry for 2–3 minutes, until just golden. Stir in the mushrooms and potatoes and fry for 1–2 minutes. Stir in 450 ml (¾ pint) of water, the porcini and their liquid, the coriander and mustard. Season with salt and pepper. Bring to the boil, reduce the heat and leave to simmer for 15 minutes.

❸ While the soup is simmering, heat the remaining butter in a separate pan. Beat in the flour and cook for 1 minute. Away from the heat, gradually beat in the milk. Return to the heat and cook over a gentle heat for 5 minutes, until thickened. Add the nutmeg and season to taste.

❹ Gently stir the white sauce into the mushroom mixture and leave to cool slightly. Blend the soup in a liquidiser or food processor and return to a clean pan. Return to the heat and cook for 2–3 minutes, until heated through. Adjust the seasoning, if needed. Serve sprinkled with extra chopped fresh coriander.

Spinaci al Lardo
Spinach and Crispy Bacon Salad

Preparation and cooking time: 15 minutes.
Freezing: not recommended. Serves 4.

I also like to add sliced raw mushrooms to this salad, to vary the flavour; in winter, I often heat through the dressing.

2 tablespoons vegetable oil
175 g (6 oz) smoked bacon, chopped
250 g (8 oz) young spinach leaves
For the Dressing:
125 ml (4 fl oz) extra-virgin olive oil

50 ml (2 fl oz) red-wine vinegar
1 teaspoon smooth mustard
50 g (2 oz) walnut pieces, crushed
salt and freshly ground black pepper

❶ Heat the oil in a frying-pan and add the bacon. Gently cook for 8–10 minutes, until crisp. Remove with a slotted spoon and drain on kitchen paper.

❷ Divide the spinach leaves between four serving plates and sprinkle over the bacon.

❸ For the dressing, place the oil, vinegar, mustard and walnuts in a bowl. Season with salt and pepper. Whisk the ingredients with a fork, until thoroughly mixed. Drizzle the dressing over the salad and serve immediately.

Insalatina Tiepida
Warm Egg Salad

Preparation and cooking time: 15 minutes.
Freezing: not recommended. Serves 4.

A delicious salad using the most basic ingredients. If you like, use a mustard dressing in place of the balsamic vinegar and coriander.

250 g (8 oz) mixed salad leaves
4 tablespoons olive oil
1 garlic clove, chopped
4 slices of white bread, crusts removed, cubed

160 g bunch fresh coriander, chopped roughly
4 tablespoons balsamic vinegar
4 eggs
freshly ground black pepper

❶ Divide the salad leaves between four serving plates. Set aside until required.

❷ Heat the oil in a large pan and add the garlic. Fry for a minute and then remove the garlic and discard. Add the bread to the oil and fry for 2–3 minutes, stirring frequently, until golden all over. Remove with a slotted spoon and drain on kitchen paper. Add the coriander and balsamic vinegar to the oil and set aside.

❸ Bring a large pan of water to the boil. Reduce to a simmer and then add the eggs; poach for 4 minutes.

❹ Gently lift the eggs out with a slotted spoon and place on the salad leaves. Sprinkle over the croûtons. Heat the dressing for 30 seconds and then spoon over the salads. Sprinkle with pepper.

Rucola e Parmigiano
Rocket and Parmesan Salad

Preparation time: 5 minutes.
Freezing: not recommended. Serves 4.

This is very trendy and always a winner at a dinner party!

2 × 40 g bags of rocket

100 g (3½ oz) piece of parmesan cheese

For the dressing:

125 ml (4 fl oz) extra-virgin olive oil

1 lemon

1 garlic clove, crushed

1 teaspoon smooth mustard

salt and freshly ground black pepper

❶ Divide the rocket leaves between four serving plates. Using a potato peeler, make thin shavings from the parmesan cheese and sprinkle over the rocket leaves.

❷ For the dressing, place the oil in a small bowl. Finely grate the lemon zest into the oil. Halve the lemon, squeeze out the juice and add the oil. Using a fork, whisk the garlic, mustard, salt and pepper into the oil mixture. Drizzle the dressing over the salad just before serving.

Patate, Radicchio e Salmone
Potato, Radicchio and Smoked Salmon Salad

Preparation and cooking time: 20 minutes.
Freezing: not recommended. Serves 4.

I like to serve this salad with Merluzzo al Crudo (Poached Cod Fillet with Tomatoes and Basil, page 68) on a nice sunny day. Sliced smoked trout or smoked salmon trimmings can be used in place of the smoked salmon, remove the skin and flake the fish over the potato salad.

500 g (1 lb) new potatoes, scrubbed

1 bunch of spring onions, chopped

1 bunch of fresh chives, snipped

leaves from 1 pot of fresh basil, chopped roughly

200 g jar of mayonnaise

25 g (1 oz) capers

3 lemons

2 radicchio heads, shredded

4 slices of smoked salmon

salt and freshly ground black pepper

❶ Cook the potatoes in a large pan of salted boiling water for 8–10 minutes, until tender. Drain and halve.

❷ Put the potatoes in a large bowl and add the spring onions, chives and basil. In a separate bowl, mix the mayonnaise with the capers and the juice from one of the lemons. Season to taste and then gently stir into the potato mixture.

❸ To assemble, divide the radicchio between four serving plates, making a pile in the centre of each. Top with the potato salad and ruffles of the smoked salmon. Sprinkle with pepper. Cut the remaining lemons into wedges and use to garnish.

Patate alle Noci
Sautéed Potatoes with Walnuts

Preparation and cooking time: 25 minutes.
Freezing: not recommended. Serves 4.

This is the perfect accompaniment to meat or liver main courses.

4 medium-sized potatoes

4 tablespoons olive oil

2 red onions, sliced

250 g (8 oz) walnut pieces

50 g (2 oz) butter

1 teaspoon freshly grated nutmeg

salt and freshly ground black pepper

❶ Put the potatoes in a large pan of salted water. Bring to the boil and cook for 8–10 minutes, until just tender. Drain the potatoes and cut them into cubes.

❷ Meanwhile, heat the oil in a large frying-pan and add the onions. Cook the onions for 5–8 minutes, until they are golden brown. Stir in the walnuts, butter, potatoes and nutmeg. Cook over a gentle heat for 5–8 minutes, until the potatoes are tender. Season to taste with salt and pepper. Serve at once.

Funghi Stroganoff
Flat Mushrooms in Cream and Mustard Sauce

Preparation and cooking time: 20 minutes.
Freezing: not recommended. Serves 4.

Halve the quantities of mushrooms, butter and cream if you plan to serve this dish as a starter, accompaniment or sauce for pasta.

16 flat mushrooms or 1 kg (2 lb) oyster
   mushrooms

2 tablespoons olive oil

2 shallots, chopped finely

1 garlic clove, chopped

150 ml (¼ pint) dry white wine

50 g (2 oz) butter

150 ml (5 fl oz) single cream

1 tablespoon English mustard

1 teaspoon paprika

salt and freshly ground black pepper

❶ If using flat mushrooms, remove the stalks and slice. Slice the mushrooms lengthways. If using oyster mushrooms, slice thickly.

❷ Heat the oil in a large frying-pan. Add the shallots and garlic and gently cook for 2–3 minutes, until golden brown. Stir in the mushrooms and cook for 5–8 minutes, until soft.

❸ Stir the wine into the mushrooms and simmer for 2 minutes. Add the butter, cream and mustard and stir well. Simmer for 5 minutes, until heated through and quite thick. Season to taste with paprika, salt and pepper. Serve at once.

Cavolfiore Romagnola
Cauliflower and Cheese Gratin

Preparation and cooking time: 25 minutes.
Freezing: recommended. Serves 4.

Serve this as an accompaniment to beef or lamb. I like the crunchy texture of cauliflower and quite often adds small, uncooked florets to salads; or I simply blanch them and mix with oil, anchovies, capers and wine vinegar.

1 medium-sized cauliflower, cut into florets
50 g (2 oz) butter
2 tablespoons plain flour
450 ml (¾ pint) milk

4 tablespoons freshly grated parmesan cheese
1 teaspoon freshly grated nutmeg
salt and freshly ground black pepper

❶ Bring a large pan of water to the boil and add the cauliflower florets. Return to the boil, reduce the heat and simmer for 10–12 minutes, until tender yet still crisp. Drain.

❷ Meanwhile, make the cheese sauce. Melt the butter in a saucepan and beat in the flour. Cook for a minute. Away from the heat, gradually beat in the milk. Return to the heat and cook for 5 minutes, stirring constantly, until the sauce thickens. Away from the heat again, mix in three-quarters of the cheese and all the nutmeg. Season to taste with salt and pepper. Preheat the grill to medium hot.

❸ Transfer the cauliflower to a gratin dish and pour over the cheese sauce. Sprinkle with the remaining parmesan cheese and extra pepper. Cook the gratin under the grill for 5 minutes, until the cheese is golden brown and bubbling. Serve immediately.

Cavolo Stufato
Braised Red Cabbage and Onions

Preparation time: 10 minutes + 15 minutes cooking.
Freezing: recommended. Serves 4.

This cabbage has a delicious caramelised flavour, making it the ideal accompaniment to a Sunday roast.

4 tablespoons olive oil
1 large onion, sliced
1 red cabbage, shredded
50 g (2 oz) raisins

4 tablespoons soft light brown sugar
2 tablespoons white-wine vinegar
6 tablespoons vegetable stock
salt and freshly ground black pepper

❶ Heat the oil in a large pan and add the onion. Gently fry the onion for 5–8 minutes, until golden brown.

❷ Stir in the cabbage, raisins, sugar, vinegar and stock. Season well with salt and pepper. Cover and simmer for 15 minutes, until the cabbage is very tender. Adjust the seasoning before serving.

Caponata all' Italiana
Italian-style Ratatouille

Preparation time: 10 minutes + 20 minutes cooking.
Freezing: recommended. Serves 4.

This dish improves in flavour when made the day before. It can also be served cold or mixed with pasta.

4 tablespoons olive oil

1 onion, chopped

2 garlic cloves, chopped

1 red pepper, de-seeded and cut into squares

1 green pepper, de-seeded and cut into squares

1 aubergine, cubed

2 courgettes, sliced

400 g can of peeled plum tomatoes

1 tablespoon tomato purée

2 bay leaves

1 tablespoon white-wine vinegar

1 teaspoon brown sugar

leaves from 1 pot of basil, chopped roughly

salt and freshly ground black pepper

❶ Heat the oil in a large pan and add the onion and garlic. Cook over a gentle heat for 2–3 minutes, until soft.

❷ Stir the peppers and aubergines into the onions and cook for 3 minutes. Add the courgettes, tomatoes, tomato purée, bay leaves, vinegar and sugar. Simmer for 20 minutes, until the vegetables are very tender and the juices reduced.

❸ Stir in the basil and season to taste with salt and pepper. Serve warm or cold.

Endive al Dolcelatte
Mixed Endives with Dolcelatte

Preparation time: 5 minutes.
Freezing: not recommended. Serves 4.

Bitter endive lettuces provide the perfect contrast to the rich, creamy Italian dolcelatte cheese. However, any blue cheese can be used for this recipe – another one of my favourites is Roquefort.

3 chicory heads, leaves separated

250 g (8 oz) dolcelatte cheese, sliced thinly

1 radicchio head, shredded

125 ml (4 fl oz) ready-made blue cheese dressing

freshly ground black pepper

❶ Arrange the chicory leaves in a circle on four serving plates. Gently place a slice of dolcelatte cheese in each leaf.

❷ Place a small pile of shredded radicchio in the centre of each plate and then drizzle the dressing on the chicory leaves with the cheese. Sprinkle with pepper to serve.

Pasta e Risotti
Pasta and Risottos

The variety of pastas is endless; there is a great difference between the fresh and dried pasta available in supermarkets – fresh pasta can taste better and cook more quickly. Allow about 150 g (5 oz) of uncooked fresh or dry pasta per person.

Rice is used quite a lot in Italian cooking. Soups, starters and desserts can all include rice and, now, there are even some ice creams made with rice! However, risotto should only be made with a risotto rice, such as arborio, which gives a creamy yet nutty texture. Allow 150 g (5 oz) of uncooked risotto rice per person.

The important point to bear in mind when cooking both rice and pasta is not to overcook them to the point of sogginess. Pasta should be cooked until it's tender but still has a slight 'bite': the Italians call this *al dente* ('to the tooth').

Farfalle ai Pomodori Secchi e Mascarpone
Pasta Bows with Sun-dried Tomatoes and Mascarpone

Preparation and cooking time: 15 minutes.
Freezing: not recommended. Serves 4.

Mascarpone cheese is a rich Italian cream cheese, which melts to a rich and simple pasta sauce in minutes. Mascarpone is also used for desserts (pages 74, 76) or simply spread on toasted bread – delicious!

500 g (1 lb) pasta bows
25 g (1 oz) butter
½ × 285 g jar of sun-dried tomatoes in oil, drained and sliced
2 garlic cloves, crushed
4 tablespoons vegetable stock
250 g (8 oz) mascarpone cheese
4 tablespoons grated parmesan cheese
leaves from 1 pot of fresh basil
salt and freshly ground black pepper

❶ Bring a large pan of salted water to the boil. Add the pasta and cook for 10 minutes until *al dente*.

❷ Meanwhile, melt the butter in a large frying-pan and add the sun-dried tomatoes and garlic. Cook gently for 2 minutes. Add the stock and mascarpone to the pan. Stir gently over the heat, until the sauce easily pours out of a spoon; add a little extra stock, if necessary.

❸ Drain the pasta and return to the pan. Add the mascarpone sauce, parmesan cheese and three-quarters of the basil leaves. Season with salt and pepper to taste. Serve with the remaining basil leaves scattered over the top.

Rigatoni alla Salsiccia
Rigatoni Pasta with Sausage Bolognese

Preparation and cooking time: 30 minutes.
Freezing: not recommended. Serves 4.

An old-fashioned dish that I remember from Christmas time, when all the fattened pig was served for our seasonal feast.

500 g (1 lb) spicy sausages

2 tablespoons olive oil

1 onion, chopped finely

1 garlic clove, chopped

150 ml (¼ pint) Italian red wine

2 extra-large tomatoes, skinned and chopped

1 tablespoon tomato purée

500 g (1 lb) rigatoni

4 tablespoons freshly grated parmesan cheese

leaves from 1 pot of fresh basil, chopped
    roughly

salt and freshly ground black pepper

❶ Bring a pan of water to the boil, add the sausages and cook for 10 minutes, until just tender. Drain and leave to cool for 5 minutes.

❷ Meanwhile, heat the oil in a large pan, add the onion and garlic and cook for 3–4 minutes, until soft. Finally chop the sausages and add to the pan, with the red wine. Bring to the boil and then leave to simmer for 5 minutes, until the wine has reduced by half. Stir in the tomatoes and tomato purée and simmer for 10 minutes, until the sauce thickens.

❸ Meanwhile, cook the pasta in a large pan of salted, boiling water for 15 minutes until *al dente*. Drain the pasta and stir it into the sausage bolognese sauce, with the parmesan cheese. Season to taste with salt and pepper. Serve immediately, sprinkled with the chopped fresh basil.

Vermicelli Cacio e Peperoni
Vermicelli with Cheese and Peppers

Preparation and cooking time: 20 minutes.
Freezing: not recommended. Serves 4.

1 each red, green and yellow peppers

8 tablespoons olive oil

1 onion, chopped

2 garlic cloves, chopped

185 g can of pitted black olives, halved

500 g (1 lb) vermicelli

150 ml (¼ pint) vegetable stock

125 g (4 oz) pecorino or parmesan cheese, grated

salt and freshly ground black pepper

❶ Slice the peppers into strips.

❷ Heat 6 tablespoons of the oil in a large frying-pan and add the peppers and onion. Cook over a moderately high heat for 8–10 minutes, until softened, stirring frequently. Stir in the garlic and black olives and season with salt and pepper. Cook for a further 1–2 minutes.

❸ Cook the vermicelli in a pan of salted, boiling water for 2–3 minutes.

❹ Drain the vermicelli and transfer to the pepper mixture. Add the stock and three-quarters of the cheese. Toss well and continue to cook for 2–3 minutes.

❺ To serve, divide the vermicelli between four warmed serving plates and drizzle with the remaining olive oil. Sprinkle with the remaining cheese and some pepper.

Penne Primavera
Penne with Mushroom Sauce

Preparation and cooking time: 25 minutes.
Freezing: not recommended. Serves 4.

2 tablespoons olive oil

1 small onion, chopped

1 garlic clove, chopped

1 kg (2 lb) button mushrooms, chopped

2 courgettes, chopped

2 extra-large tomatoes

leaves from 1 pot of fresh basil, chopped roughly

300 g tub of wild-mushroom sauce

150 ml (5 fl oz) single cream

500 g (1 lb) penne

salt and freshly ground black pepper

❶ Heat the oil in a large pan. Add the onion and cook for 3–5 minutes, until golden. Add the garlic, mushrooms and courgettes and cook for 10 minutes.

❷ Meanwhile, blanch the tomatoes in a pan of boiling water for 2–3 minutes. Drain and refresh under cold water. Skin the tomatoes and then roughly chop the flesh. Add the tomatoes and three-quarters of the basil to the courgette mixture, stir well and cook for a further 10 minutes.

❸ Add the mushroom sauce and cream and cook for 5 minutes. Season to taste.

❹ Cook the pasta in a pan of salted, boiling water for 10–12 minutes. Drain and transfer to a large bowl, spoon over the vegetable sauce and sprinkle with the remaining basil.

Gnocchi al Dolcelatte
Gnocchi with Dolcelatte Cheese Sauce
Preparation and cooking time: 30 minutes.
Freezing: not recommended. Serves 4.

Gnocchi are small potato dumplings that cook in minutes. They can be served with all pasta sauces, especially fresh carbonara sauce, which is available ready-made in Sainsbury's. This dolcelatte-cheese recipe is one of my favourites; however, for something a little lighter, try chopped fresh tomatoes, basil and garlic.

50 g (2 oz) butter
2 tablespoons plain flour
600 ml (1 pint) milk
½ teaspoon freshly grated nutmeg
250 g (8 oz) dolcelatte cheese, cubed

1 teaspoon olive oil
2 × 500 g packets of fresh gnocchi
4 tablespoons freshly grated parmesan cheese
salt and freshly ground black pepper

❶ Heat half the butter in a pan, until foaming. Add the flour and beat over the heat for a minute. Away from the heat, gradually add the milk, beating well between each addition. Return to the heat and cook gently for 3–5 minutes, stirring constantly, until the sauce thickens. Season with nutmeg, salt and pepper to taste. Set the sauce aside, until required.

❷ Bring a large pan of salted water to the boil. In a separate pan, gently heat the remaining butter, dolcelatte cheese and 2–3 tablespoons of water, until the cheese melts, stirring frequently.

❸ Add the olive oil to the salted, boiling water and then add the gnocchi and cook for 2–3 minutes, until they rise to the surface. Remove the gnocchi with a draining spoon and add to the dolcelatte mixture, gradually stirring in half of the sauce, too. Preheat the grill to medium hot.

❹ Transfer the gnocchi mixture to a large gratin dish and spoon over the remaining sauce. Sprinkle over the grated parmesan cheese and grill for 3–5 minutes, until golden and bubbling. Sprinkle with pepper to serve.

Tagliatelle al Pesto Rosso
Tagliatelle with Red Pesto
Preparation and cooking time: 20 minutes.
Freezing: not recommended. Serves 4.

It's extremely easy to make your own pesto and this one, using red basil leaves, is delicious. However, if time is extremely short, use two jars of ready-made red pesto. This is a great recipe for friends; if you like, omit the cream for a lighter result.

For the Red Pesto:
3 pots of fresh red basil
1 tablespoon chopped fresh flat-leaf parsley
3 garlic cloves, crushed
2 tablespoons pine kernels
4 tablespoons freshly grated parmesan cheese
150 ml (¼ pint) extra-virgin olive oil

For the Pasta:
500 g (1 lb) tagliatelle
25 g (1 oz) butter
300 ml (10 fl oz) single cream (optional)
salt and freshly ground black pepper
fresh red basil leaves, to garnish

❶ For the pesto, remove the basil leaves from the stalks and finely chop. Place the leaves in a pestle and mortar, with the parsley, garlic, pine kernels and parmesan cheese. Add salt and pepper. Pound the mixture until smooth, gradually adding the oil. The pesto should have a fine, grainy texture. Alternatively, make the pesto in a food processor. Blend the herbs with the pine kernels and then add the garlic, cheese and seasoning. While the machine is still running, gradually add the olive oil, in a thin, steady stream.

❷ Cook the tagliatelle in a large pan of boiling, salted water for 8–10 minutes, until *al dente*. Drain the pasta, reserving a little of the cooking liquid.
❸ Meanwhile, in a separate pan, put the butter, cream (if using) and pesto. Stir well and simmer for 3–4 minutes, until slightly reduced. Add the drained pasta and toss to mix; if the pasta mixture looks a little dry, add some of the reserved cooking liquid. Serve immediately, sprinkled with red basil leaves.

Risotto ai Funghi
Field and Wild Mushroom Risotto

Preparation and cooking time: 30 minutes.
Freezing: not recommended. Serves 6.

If you like, use dried porcini mushrooms in place of the wild mushrooms. Soak two 10 g packets of dried porcini mushrooms in 150 ml (¼ pint) of hot water for at least 10–15 minutes. Drain, reserving the liquid, and chop the porcini. Add the porcini and reserved liquid halfway through cooking the risotto. It's important to stir the risotto constantly while it cooks.

4 tablespoons olive oil

1 onion, chopped finely

1 garlic clove, crushed

375 g (12 oz) risotto rice

300 ml (½ pint) dry white wine

1 kg (2 lb) flat mushrooms, sliced

1.2 litres (2 pints) hot vegetable stock

500 g (1 lb) mixed wild mushrooms, e.g.
  oyster, trumpet, shiitake

2 tablespoons chopped fresh flat-leaf parsley

125 g (4 oz) freshly grated parmesan cheese

125 g (4 oz) butter

❶ Heat the oil in a large pan and add the onion. Cook gently for 2–3 minutes, until soft. Add the garlic and cook for a minute. Add the rice, wine and flat mushrooms and then cook for 5–8 minutes, stirring frequently, until the mushrooms are soft and the wine has evaporated.

❷ Add a ladleful of the stock to the mushroom mixture and simmer, stirring constantly, until the liquid has been absorbed. Continue adding the stock and simmering until half the stock has been added.

❸ Chop three-quarters of the wild mushrooms and add to the risotto mixture. Continue adding the stock and simmering until the rice is tender; this should take about 20–25 minutes in total.

❹ Season the risotto with salt and pepper to taste. Stir in the parsley, parmesan cheese and three-quarters of the butter. The consistency of the risotto should be slightly runny.

❺ Heat the remaining butter in a frying-pan and add the reserved wild mushrooms; fry for 2–3 minutes. To serve, spoon the risotto on to warmed serving plates and top with the fried wild mushrooms.

Risotto al Gambero
Prawn and Spinach Risotto

Preparation and cooking time: 30 minutes.
Freezing: not recommended. Serves 6.

I know all the rules about 'no parmesan with fish' but I love it with this risotto. Do not hesitate to add any other vegetables you may have at home when making this recipe.

2 tablespoons olive oil

1 onion, chopped finely

1 garlic clove, crushed

6 raw Mediterranean prawns, peeled and chopped

375 g (12 oz) risotto rice

150 ml (¼ pint) dry white wine

1.2 litres (2 pints) hot fish stock

1 kg (2 lb) young spinach leaves

2 tablespoons freshly grated parmesan cheese

125 g (4 oz) butter

salt and freshly ground black pepper

6 Mediterranean prawns, peeled but with shells on tails left intact, to garnish

❶ Heat the oil in a large pan and add the onion. Cook for 2–3 minutes, until soft. Add the garlic and prawns and cook for 3–4 minutes, stirring frequently.

❷ Add the rice and wine and cook for 5–8 minutes, until the wine evaporates, stirring constantly. Add a ladleful of fish stock to the rice and simmer until the liquid has been absorbed, stirring constantly. Continue adding the stock in this way until three-quarters has been added.

❸ Stir in the spinach leaves and the remaining stock. Simmer, stirring constantly, until the rice is tender. This should take about 20–25 minutes in total. Season with salt and pepper to taste. Stir in the parmesan cheese and three-quarters of the butter. The consistency should be slightly runny.

❹ Halve the prawns, lengthways, leaving the prawns intact at the tail end. Heat the remaining butter in a frying-pan and add the prawns; fry for 2–3 minutes on each side until golden brown. Divide the risotto between six warmed serving plates and top each with a prawn. Sprinkle with extra pepper to serve.

Linguine Capesante
Linguine with Scallops and Leeks

Preparation and cooking time: 20 minutes.
Freezing: not recommended. Serves 4.

King scallops can be expensive, however, the smaller queen or China bay scallops can also be used. Other shellfish, such as mussels and prawns, or white fish, such as cod or haddock, can also be used.

500 g (1 lb) linguine

4 tablespoons olive oil

2 leeks, chopped finely

2 garlic cloves, crushed

8 king scallops, halved

150 ml (¼ pint) dry white wine

150 ml (¼ pint) hot vegetable stock

2 tablespoons chopped fresh basil

2 tablespoons chopped fresh flat-leaf parsley

salt and freshly ground black pepper

❶ Bring a large pan of salted water to the boil. Add the linguine and cook for 8–10 minutes until *al dente*.

❷ Meanwhile, heat the oil in a large pan and add the leeks and garlic. Cook gently for 3–5 minutes, until soft. Add the scallops and cook for 2–3 minutes on each side, until golden. Add the wine and half of the stock and bring to the boil. Reduce the heat and simmer for 5 minutes.

❸ Drain the pasta and add to the leek mixture; toss well to mix. Add half the herbs and a little extra stock, if required. Season with salt and pepper to taste; cook for 1–2 minutes, to heat through. To serve, transfer the linguine mixture to warmed serving plates and garnish with the remaining basil and parsley.

Carne e Pesce
Meat and Fish

Veal became very popular in Italy because the beef available there was very tough, unlike the beef available in the UK. The veal recipes in this chapter can be made with pork or lamb; they will, of course, taste slightly different but they will still be very delicious.

Rabbit and chicken used to be the staple meats in most Italian villages, as they were very cheap to rear and easy to keep in the backyard. They are still very popular in many southern villages. Rabbit and chicken dishes in Italian cookery are endless and all packed with succulent flavours.

Fish cookery in Italy has always been popular in restaurants and at home in fishing villages, because fish was cheap. In England, cooking fish at home is not as popular as it should be. Make the most of the fish available in supermarkets – all the hard work has been done for you; keep it simple and you really will notice how effortless it is to cook fish. The easiest and tastiest way to serve fish is to coat it with olive oil, lemon juice and seasoning and then grill, barbecue or bake. It's also very healthy!

Filetti di Pollo Pizzaiola
Chicken Fillets with Tomatoes and Wine Sauce

Preparation and cooking time: 30 minutes.
Freezing: not recommended. Serves 4.

This is very tasty served with a little Risotto al Funghi (Field and Wild Mushroom Risotto, page 44).

50 g (2 oz) butter
1 garlic clove, crushed
4 boneless, skinless chicken breasts, sliced thinly
500 g (1 lb) plum tomatoes, chopped
250 ml (8 fl oz) dry white wine

4 anchovy fillets in oil, drained and chopped
1 teaspoon dried chopped oregano
125 g (4 oz) pitted black olives, halved
salt and freshly ground black pepper
chopped fresh mixed herbs, to garnish

❶ Heat the butter in a pan, add the garlic and fry for a minute. Add the chicken slices and cook for 3 minutes on both sides, until golden brown.
❷ Add the tomatoes and wine to the chicken and simmer for 2 minutes. Stir in the anchovies, oregano and olives to the pan and season with pepper. Simmer for 10 minutes.
❸ To serve, arrange the chicken fillets on warmed serving plates and then spoon over the tomato and wine sauce. Sprinkle with the chopped fresh herbs to serve.

Tacchino alla Frutta
Turkey Escalopes with Berries

Preparation and cooking time: 30 minutes.
Freezing: not recommended. Serves 4.

This is not a traditional Italian recipe but it is one I enjoy a lot. If you like, use chicken or veal and serve with Caponata all' Italiana (Italian-style Ratatouille, page 32).

125 g (4 oz) butter
1 kg (2 lb) fresh or frozen mixed berries,
  thawed if necessary
150 ml (¼ pint) orange juice
4 tablespoons olive oil
1 large onion, cut into thin wedges

25 g (1 oz) soft light brown sugar
2 teaspoons wine vinegar
1 tablespoon plain flour
4 turkey escalopes
salt and freshly ground black pepper

❶ Heat 25 g (1 oz) of the butter in a pan and add the berries and orange juice. Allow to simmer for 15 minutes; the berries should be quite mushy and syrupy.

❷ Meanwhile, heat a little of the oil in a frying-pan with 50 g (2 oz) of the remaining butter; add the onions. Fry for 5 minutes, until the onions are golden brown. Stir in the sugar and cook gently for 8–10 minutes, until the onions have caramelised. Stir in the vinegar and heat for a minute.

❸ Meanwhile, season the flour with salt and pepper. Heat the remaining oil and butter in a large frying-pan. Coat each turkey escalope with the seasoned flour and add to the pan. Cook for 5 minutes until golden brown on both sides and cooked through. Remove and drain on kitchen paper.

❹ To serve, place the turkey escalopes on large, warmed serving plates. Spoon some of the caramelised onions on one side of the escalope and the berry sauce on the other. Serve immediately.

Pollo Ripieno
Stuffed Chicken with Ham and Leeks

Preparation and cooking time: 25 minutes.
Freezing: not recommended. Serves 4.

For extra flavour, I like to use free-range chickens. This is a very simple main course. Serve with sautéed potatoes and a crisp salad.

2 tablespoons olive oil
2 leeks, chopped finely
4 slices of ham, chopped
4 × 175 g (6 oz) chicken breasts
50 g (2 oz) butter

1 large onion, chopped finely
150 ml (¼ pint) dry white wine
6 tablespoons chopped fresh flat-leaf parsley
salt and freshly ground black pepper

❶ Preheat the oven to Gas Mark 5/190°C/375°F. Heat the oil in a frying-pan and add the leeks. Fry the leeks for 3 minutes, until soft. Add the ham to the leeks and cook for a minute. Remove from the heat and season with salt and pepper.

❷ Using a sharp knife, gently cut a pocket in the side of each chicken breast. Fill each chicken pocket with the leek and ham filling and then close and secure with a cocktail stick. Place the chicken in the frying-pan and cook in the leek and ham juices for 3 minutes on each side,

until golden brown. Transfer to a baking tray and bake for 15 minutes.

❸ Meanwhile, melt the butter in a clean frying-pan and add the onion. Cook for 5 minutes, until golden. Add the wine and three-quarters of the parsley. Simmer for 5–8 minutes, until the onions are very tender and the juices reduced.

❹ To serve, place the chicken on warmed serving plates and remove the cocktail sticks. Spoon over the onion sauce. Sprinkle with the remaining parsley to serve.

Coniglio ai Funghi
Rabbit and Mushroom Casserole

Preparation and cooking time: 30 minutes.
Freezing: recommended. Serves 4.

Rabbit used to be poor man's food. However, these days, rabbit is quite a delicacy; therefore, serve this flavoursome casserole for special occasions. If you have time, marinate the rabbit in the wine and herbs for two hours at room temperature.

6 tablespoons olive oil

1 red onion, chopped

4 garlic cloves, bashed to break the skins

4 tablespoons plain flour

1 kg (2 lb) rabbit meat, cut into chunks, or
    1 whole rabbit, boned

300 ml (½ pint) dry white wine

625 g (1¼ lb) flat mushrooms, sliced

3–4 sprigs of fresh rosemary

125 g (4 oz) pitted green olives

4 bay leaves

1 fresh chilli, de-seeded and chopped finely

For the Mash:

1 kg (2 lb) sweet potatoes

2 tablespoons milk

50 g (2 oz) butter

1 teaspoon freshly grated nutmeg

salt and freshly ground black pepper

fresh rosemary sprigs, to garnish

❶ Heat the oil in a heavy-based roasting tin or casserole dish. Add the onion and garlic and cook for 3–5 minutes, until just golden.

❷ Meanwhile, season the flour with salt and pepper and use to coat the rabbit all over. Add the rabbit to the pan and cook for 5 minutes, until golden brown all over. Add the wine and cook for 2 minutes. Add the mushrooms and cook for a further 5 minutes. Add the rosemary, olives, bay leaves and chilli. Season with salt and pepper, cover and simmer for 25 minutes.

❸ Meanwhile, cook the sweet potatoes in a pan of salted, boiling water and cook for 15 minutes, until very tender. Drain and transfer to a large bowl. Add the milk, butter and nutmeg and mash to a purée. Season to taste with salt and pepper. Set aside and keep warm.

❹ Divide the mash between four warmed serving plates. Spoon over the rabbit casserole. Garnish with extra rosemary sprigs to serve.

Cotolette di Maiale al Lardo
Wrapped Pork Chops with Mustard Sauce

Preparation and cooking time: 30 minutes.
Freezing: not recommended. Serves 4.

Pancetta is Italian bacon; it is available smoked or unsmoked and can be used to replace bacon in any recipe. Pancetta has a much stronger flavour than bacon. Pancetta or bacon wrapped around meat helps to keep it extra juicy and succulent. Serve these chops with Cavolo Stufato (Braised Red Cabbage and Onions, page 30).

4 rashers of bacon or pancetta, de-rinded

4 loin pork chops

4 tablespoons olive oil

1 onion, chopped

150 ml (¼ pint) dry white wine

150 ml (¼ pint) vegetable stock

2 tablespoons chopped fresh flat-leaf parsley

2 tablespoons chopped fresh rosemary

2 tablespoons chopped fresh sage

1 tablespoon English mustard

150 ml (5 fl oz) single cream

❶ Preheat the oven to Gas Mark 6/200°C/400°F. Using the blunt side of a knife, scrape along the bacon rashers until they have almost doubled in length. Trim most of the fat from pork chops and then cut the remaining fat at regular intervals. Wrap the bacon around the chops.

❷ Heat the oil in a large frying-pan and add the pork chops. Cook for 3–4 minutes on each side, to brown. Remove the chops and set aside. Stir the onion into the pan juices and fry for 5 minutes, until golden. Return the chops to the pan and add the wine and stock. Bring to the boil and cook for 6 minutes.

❸ Transfer the chops to the oven and bake for 10 minutes, until cooked through and just beginning to brown.

❹ Return the pan to the heat, stir in the herbs, mustard and cream and season to taste with salt and pepper. Simmer for 5 minutes. To serve, spoon the sauce on to warmed plates, and top with the chops.

Vitello Valdostana
Veal Escalopes with Parma Ham and Mozzarella

Preparation and cooking time: 25 minutes.
Freezing: not recommended. Serves 4.

This dish reminds me of my first restaurant, where it was a big favourite with the Americans; they called it 'veal Parmigiana' because you also sprinkle it with grated parmesan when serving. If you like, use pork or beef in place of the veal; escalopes or fillets are very tender cuts that are suitable.

4 veal escalopes

4 tablespoons plain flour

4 tablespoons olive oil

50 g (2 oz) butter

150 ml (¼ pint) dry white wine

4 slices of Parma ham

200 g (7 oz) mozzarella cheese, sliced

2 extra-large tomatoes, sliced

4 tablespoons chopped fresh basil

salt and freshly ground black pepper

grated parmesan cheese, to serve

❶ Season the veal escalopes with salt and pepper and then coat them all over with flour. Heat the oil in a large frying-pan and add the escalopes. Cook for 4 minutes on each side. Remove and set aside. Preheat the grill to medium hot.

❷ Add the butter and wine to the pan juices and simmer for 3–4 minutes, until reduced. Return the escalopes to the pan and top with the ham, mozzarella and tomatoes. Spoon over some of the juices.

❸ Place the pan under the grill and cook for 5–8 minutes, until the tomatoes are tender and the mozzarella has melted. Sprinkle with the basil and parmesan cheese to serve.

Filetto al Pomodoro Affumicato
Lamb or Beef Fillets with Tomato and Garlic Bread

Preparation and cooking time: 25 minutes.
Freezing: not recommended. Serves 4.

This dish tastes great made with either lamb or beef fillets, though lamb fillet is considerably cheaper than beef.

500 g (1 lb) lamb or beef fillets

4 tablespoons olive oil

2 extra-large tomatoes

4 rashers of smoked bacon, de-rinded and chopped

2 garlic cloves, crushed

1 ciabatta loaf, sliced horizontally and then halved widthways

2 tablespoons brown sugar

salt and freshly ground black pepper

❶ Preheat the oven to Gas Mark 6/200°C/400°F. Divide the lamb or beef fillets into four. Heat half the oil in a heavy-based roasting tin and cook the fillets for 3 minutes on each side. Transfer to the oven and cook for 10 minutes.

❷ Meanwhile, blanch the tomatoes in boiling water for 2 minutes. Drain under cold water. Slip off the skins and chop the flesh. Fry the bacon in its own fat for 3–5 minutes, until almost crisp. Drain on kitchen paper. In a small bowl, mix the bacon and tomatoes.

❸ Preheat the grill to hot. For the garlic toast, mix the remaining oil with the garlic and spoon or brush it over the cut side of each ciabatta slice. Place on a grill rack and toast under the grill, until golden. Set aside.

❹ Slice the fillets and sprinkle the sugar over the slices. Place under the grill and cook for 2–3 minutes, until the sugar has dissolved. Top each toast with a piece of fillet and spoon over the tomato mixture. Serve immediately.

Fegato al Lardo
Lamb's Liver with Bacon and Caramelised Onions

Preparation and cooking time: 30 minutes.
Freezing: not recommended. Serves 4.

Pure flavour on a plate, and a complete course in just 30 minutes! Chicken livers or calves' liver may also be used – depending on the budget.

3 tablespoons olive oil

50 g (2 oz) butter

1 large onion, cut into wedges

1 tablespoon soft light brown sugar

1 tablespoon honey

4 rashers smoked bacon, de-rinded and
   chopped

750 g (1½ lb) lambs' liver, sliced

150 ml (¼ pint) dry white wine

1 tablespoon plain flour

For the Garlic and Chilli Spinach:

2 tablespoons olive oil

2 garlic cloves, chopped finely

2 fresh red chillies, de-seeded and chopped
   finely

1 kg (2 lb) young spinach leaves

salt and freshly ground black pepper

❶ Heat half the oil in a frying-pan and add half the butter. Stir in the onion, sugar and honey. Cover and cook the onion for 10 minutes, until golden brown and caramelised.

❷ Meanwhile, heat the remaining oil in a separate frying-pan. Add the bacon and cook for 3–5 minutes. Stir in the liver and cook for 8–10 minutes, until browned all over. Stir in the wine and cook over a high heat, to reduce the wine. Add the remaining butter and the flour. Cook over a gentle heat to thicken a little.

❸ For the garlic and chilli spinach, heat the oil in a large pan. Add the garlic and chilli and fry for 1 minute. Stir in the spinach and cook for 3–5 minutes, until the spinach just begins to wilt.

❹ To serve, spoon the spinach on to four warmed serving plates. Add the liver and bacon and, finally, the caramelised onions. Serve immediately.

Agnello Stufato
Quick Lamb Stew

Preparation and cooking time: 30 minutes.
Freezing: recommended. Serves 4.

2 tablespoons olive oil

1 large onion, sliced

8 shallots, halved

1 small aubergine, cut into large chunks

250 g (8 oz) button mushrooms

1 red pepper, de-seeded and cut into chunks

750 g (1½ lb) lamb fillet, cut into chunks

300 ml (½ pint) red wine

1 bay leaf

1 fresh sage sprig

1 fresh rosemary sprig

400 g can of chopped tomatoes

1 tablespoon tomato purée

1 tablespoon smooth mustard

salt and freshly ground black pepper

❶ Heat the olive oil in a large, deep pan and add the onion, shallots, aubergine, mushrooms and pepper. Cook for 5 minutes, until the onion and shallots are golden brown. Stir the lamb into the pan and cook for 5 minutes, until browned.

❷ Stir in the wine, herbs, chopped tomatoes and tomato purée. Simmer for 20 minutes, until tender.

❸ Add the mustard and season to taste. Simmer for 5 minutes and serve at once.

Cotolette di Agnello alla Milanese
Lamb Cutlets in Herbed Breadcrumbs

Preparation and cooking time: 30 minutes.
Freezing: not recommended. Serves 4.

Lamb cutlets are tender, flavoursome and very well priced. Serve with a crisp salad or plain pasta tossed with olive oil and chopped tomatoes.

4 tablespoons chopped fresh rosemary

4 tablespoons chopped fresh mint

4 tablespoons chopped fresh basil

1 teaspoon dried oregano

200 g packet of breadcrumbs

3 eggs, beaten

25 g (1 oz) plain flour

12 lamb cutlets

oil, for shallow-frying

salt and freshly ground black pepper

lemon wedges, to serve

❶ Mix the herbs with the breadcrumbs on a plate and season. Beat the eggs in a shallow bowl. On a separate plate, spread the flour and season with pepper.

❷ Coat the cutlets first with flour, then dip them in the egg and finally in the breadcrumb mixture. Heat enough oil in a large frying-pan for shallow-frying.

❸ Add the cutlets to the oil, in two batches, if necessary. Cook for 5–8 minutes on each side. Remove with a fish slice and drain on kitchen paper; keep warm while you cook the remaining cutlets. Serve with wedges of lemon.

Razza al Burro e Salvia
Skate with Sage Butter

Preparation and cooking time: 30 minutes.
Freezing: not recommended. Serves 4.

2 × 350 g (12 oz) skate wings or 4 × 175 g (6 oz) skate wings

3 tablespoons plain flour

4 tablespoons olive oil

125 g (4 oz) butter

15 g packet of fresh sage, leaves removed from stalks

180 g jar of capers, drained

150 ml (¼ pint) dry white wine

salt and freshly ground black pepper

❶ Preheat the oven to Gas Mark 6/200°C/400°F. Season the skate wings with salt and pepper and then coat both sides with the flour. Heat the oil and half the butter in a large frying-pan and add the skate (you may need to cook the skate in batches). Cook the skate for 3 minutes on each side, until golden brown. Remove with a fish slice and drain on kitchen paper; transfer to a baking tray. Place the fish in the oven and bake for 15 minutes, until crisp.

❷ Melt the remaining butter in a clean pan. Add the sage, capers and wine and season. Simmer for 2–3 minutes.

❸ To serve, place the skate on warmed serving plates and spoon over the sage butter. Serve immediately.

Merluzzo al Crudo
Poached Cod Fillet with Tomatoes and Basil

Preparation and cooking time: 15 minutes.
Freezing: not recommended. Serves 4.

1 carrot, chopped roughly

1 spring onion, chopped roughly

1 celery stick, chopped roughly

juice from 1 lemon

2 tablespoons olive oil

4 × 175 g (6 oz) cod fillets, skinned

1 extra-large tomato

2 garlic cloves, chopped finely

2 shallots, chopped finely

leaves from 1 pot of fresh basil, chopped

❶ Put the carrot, spring onion, celery, lemon juice and 1 tablespoon of the olive oil in a large frying-pan. Add enough water to poach the fish. Bring the water to the boil and then gently ease the fish into the pan. Return to the boil, reduce the heat and simmer for 8–10 minutes, until the fish is cooked through.

❷ Blanch the tomato in a separate pan of boiling water for 2 minutes. Drain and refresh under cold water. Skin and roughly chop the flesh. Place the tomato in a small bowl, with the garlic, shallots, basil and the remaining olive oil. Gently toss to mix and season.

❸ To serve, gently lift the cod from the pan with a fish slice and drain on kitchen paper. Then place the fish on warmed serving plates and top with the tomato mixture. Sprinkle with extra pepper.

Dolci
Desserts

Traditionally, Italian desserts require time, care and attention; however, the recipes in this chapter require none of these. I've done all the careful work for you and created luscious desserts that can be prepared at home in under 30 minutes.

Alternatively, finish off your meal in typical Italian style with fresh fruit or fruit salad, well chilled Vino Santo (Italian dessert wine) and *cantuccini biscotti* (almond biscuits) to dip in the wine.

Mele Farcite con Amaretti
Stuffed Baked Apples with Amaretti

Preparation: 10 minutes + 25 minutes cooking.
Freezing: not recommended. Serves 4.

Use small dessert apples, like Braeburn or Cox's, to make this dessert. If very small apples are available, use 2–3 for each serving.

50 g (2 oz) unsalted butter

4 red-skinned dessert apples

50 g (2 oz) amaretti biscuits, crushed roughly

2 tablespoons sultanas

1 tablespoon raisins

4 tablespoons clear honey

For the Vanilla Sauce:

150 ml (5 fl oz) whipping cream

2 tablespoons icing sugar

½ teaspoon vanilla essence

2 tablespoons Calvados or brandy

fresh mint sprigs, to decorate

icing sugar, to dust

❶ Preheat the oven to Gas Mark 5/190°C/ 375°F. Lightly butter an ovenproof dish with some of the butter. Using a small, sharp knife, score the apples around the middle. Using a corer, remove and discard both the stalk and core from each apple and then, using the point of a small knife, enlarge the centres a little more. Place the apples in the buttered dish.

❷ In a small bowl, mix the amaretti biscuits with the sultanas, raisins and half the honey. Spoon into the apple cavities. Dice the remaining butter and place on the apples. Bake the apples for 20 minutes.

❸ Meanwhile, make the sauce. Place the whipping cream, icing sugar, vanilla essence and Calvados or brandy in a large bowl and whisk until soft peaks form. Cover with clingfilm and chill until required.

❹ Drizzle the remaining honey over the apples and return to the oven for a further 5 minutes, until the apples are tender and the honey is just beginning to caramelise. Divide the apples between individual serving plates and spoon some of the cream next to each apple. Decorate with fresh mint sprigs and dust with icing sugar to serve.

Ananas alla Griglia
Grilled Fresh Pineapple

Preparation and cooking time: 15 minutes.
Freezing: not recommended. Serves 4.

Warm or grilled fresh pineapple with delicious lemon ice cream looks and tastes stunning.

1 large pineapple
4 tablespoons soft light brown sugar

Luscious Lemon Meringue ice cream or other lemon ice cream
chocolate curls, to decorate

❶ Remove the top and base from the pineapple. Then, holding it upright, peel, removing the eyes at the same time. Cut into four large rounds and then remove the core with a small knife. Slice the pineapple. Preheat the grill to medium hot.

❷ Place on a baking tray and sprinkle with the sugar. Grill for 5 minutes, until the sugar melts and the pineapple caramelises.

❸ Arrange on four serving plates and add 1–2 small scoops of ice cream. Decorate with chocolate curls and serve at once.

Crema di Ricotta
Ricotta Cream with Raspberry Coulis

Preparation and cooking time: 20 minutes.
Freezing: not recommended. Serves 4.

500 g (1 lb) fresh raspberries
1–2 tablespoons icing sugar
3 tablespoons orange juice
250 g (8 oz) tub of ricotta cheese
150 ml (5 fl oz) double cream
25 g (1 oz) mixed candied peel

25 g (1 oz) plain chocolate, chopped
1 tablespoon chopped candied angelica
2 egg whites
50 g (2 oz) caster sugar
fresh mint or lemon balm sprigs, to decorate

❶ Place three-quarters of the raspberries in a small pan, with the icing sugar and orange juice. Heat gently, until the sugar dissolves and then leave to simmer for 5–8 minutes, until mushy.

❷ Meanwhile, place the ricotta in a bowl and beat in the cream, mixed peel, chocolate and angelica. In a separate bowl, whisk the egg whites until soft peaks form. Gradually whisk in the caster sugar, a tablespoon at a time, beating well

between each addition. The mixture should be stiff and glossy. Fold into the ricotta with a large metal spoon.

❸ Push the raspberry mixture through a sieve. Divide the raspberry coulis between four individual dessert plates. Using two tablespoons the same size, shape the ricotta cream into ovals and place three on each plate. Decorate with the remaining raspberries and mint or lemon balm sprigs and serve at once.

Torta di Mascarpone alle Fragole
Mascarpone and Strawberry Tart
Preparation: 10 minutes + 20 minutes cooking + cooling.
Freezing: not recommended. Serves 6.

Make the most of the pastries now available in supermarkets. They're available fresh or frozen: allow enough time to thaw, if frozen.

250 g (8 oz) sweet shortcrust pastry, thawed
   if frozen
250 g (8 oz) tub of mascarpone cheese
2 tablespoons icing sugar

300 ml (10 fl oz) whipping cream
500 g (1 lb) strawberries, hulled
2 tablespoons strawberry jam, sieved

❶ Preheat the oven to Gas Mark 6/200°C/ 400°F. Place a baking tray in the oven, to preheat. Thinly roll out the pastry on a lightly floured surface until it is large enough to line a 20 cm (8-inch) round, fluted, greased tart tin. Line the tin and trim the sides. Prick the pastry all over with a fork.

❷ Line the pastry case with greaseproof paper or foil and baking beans. Bake blind for 15 minutes. Remove the beans and lining and bake for a further 5 minutes, until the pastry is golden brown. Leave until cold.

❸ Meanwhile, make the filling. In a bowl, beat the mascarpone with the sugar and then add 4 tablespoons of the cream, to loosen it a little. In a separate bowl, whisk the remaining cream, until soft peaks form. Fold the cream into the mascarpone, using a large metal spoon.

❹ Remove the pastry case from the tart tin and place on a serving plate or board. Fill the pastry case with the mascarpone cream, levelling the surface with the back of a metal spoon. Arrange the strawberries on top. Gently heat the strawberry jam with 2 tablespoons of water and then brush over the fruit, to glaze. Serve at once.

Quick Tiramisú

Preparation time: 15 minutes + 30 minutes standing.
Freezing: not recommended. Serves 4.

This is the ultimate Italian dessert of rich creamy mascarpone layered with coffee and cocoa – unbeatable!

4 eggs, separated

1 teaspoon vanilla essence

50 g (2 oz) caster sugar

125 g (4 oz) mascarpone cheese

600 ml (1 pint) double cream

300 ml (½ pint) hot strong black coffee

1 tablespoon Marsala wine

1 tablespoon coffee liqueur, e.g. Tia Maria

12 sponge finger biscuits

2 tablespoons cocoa powder

grated chocolate, to decorate

❶ Put the egg yolks in a large bowl, with the vanilla essence and half the sugar, and whisk until light and fluffy. Beat in the mascarpone, until smooth. In a separate bowl, whip the cream until soft peaks form. Using a large metal spoon, fold the cream into the mascarpone mixture. In a grease-free bowl, whisk the egg whites, with the remaining sugar, until stiff and glossy. Fold into the cream mixture.

❷ Spread half of the mascarpone mixture in a 1.2-litre (2-pint) shallow serving dish.

❸ In a large bowl, mix the coffee, Marsala wine and coffee liqueur. Dip half the sponge finger biscuits in the coffee mixture, one by one, and then arrange over the mascarpone mixture. Repeat the layers, finishing with a heavy coating of cocoa powder.

❹ Allow the tiramisú to stand for 30 minutes before serving. Spoon the tiramisú into individual serving bowls or sundae glasses and sprinkle with grated chocolate to serve.

Zabaglione

Preparation and cooking time: 20 minutes.
Freezing: not recommended. Serves 2.

A warm, syllabub-style dessert that just melts in your mouth. This classic Italian dessert must be made just before it is required and served warm.

3 egg yolks

1 tablespoon caster sugar

75 ml (3 fl oz) white wine

100 ml (3½ fl oz) Marsala wine

sponge finger biscuits, to serve

❶ Place all the ingredients in a large, heatproof bowl, set over a pan of very gently simmering water. Using an electric whisk or balloon whisk, whisk the egg-yolk mixture for 5–10 minutes, until the mixture has almost tripled in volume and is well combined. Make sure the water in the pan does not boil too fiercely, as heat may cook the egg yolks.

❷ Spoon the zabaglione into two individual serving glasses and serve immediately, with sponge finger biscuits.

Crêpes con Gelato e Frutta
Sweet Crêpes with Ice Cream and Bananas
Preparation and cooking time: 20 minutes.
Freezing: not recommended. Serves 6.

The good thing about crêpes is that they can be made beforehand and frozen. Simply thaw them, re-heat them in a pan or the oven, if you want them warm, and fill them with whatever is at hand.

3 tablespoons milk

2 eggs

4 tablespoons plain flour, sifted

1 tablespoon oil

75 g (3 oz) butter

2 tablespoons brown sugar

4 tablespoons raisins

4 bananas, sliced

6 scoops of vanilla ice cream

melted plain chocolate, to decorate

❶ For the crêpe batter, put the milk and eggs in a bowl and beat with a hand whisk. Whisk in the flour. Heat the oil with 25 g (1 oz) of the butter, until the butter melts, and then whisk into the flour mixture. Strain the batter through a sieve into a jug, to remove any lumps.

❷ Heat a small frying-pan until hot. Add a drop of oil and a little butter to the pan and swirl round to coat. Add enough batter to coat the base of the pan and cook for 2–3 minutes, until the base is golden. Flip the crêpe over and cook for a further 1–2 minutes. Transfer to greaseproof paper to drain. Repeat with the remaining batter, to make six crêpes in total.

❸ For the filling, melt the remaining butter in a large frying-pan and add the sugar and raisins; heat gently for the sugar to dissolve. Add the bananas and cook for 4–5 minutes, until the bananas are very tender. Place one of the crêpes on a clean surface and spoon some of the bananas on a quarter of the crêpe. Fold the crêpe in half and then in half again, to create a cone shape. Repeat with the remaining filling and crêpes.

❹ Divide the crêpes between six serving plates and add a scoop of vanilla ice cream. Drizzle over the warm, melted chocolate, to serve.

Index